The Power of Positive Words

90 DAY MAKEOVER FOR YOUR LIFE

Jim Kibler

THE POWER OF POSITIVE WORDS
Copyright © 2018 Jim Kibler

ACKNOWLEDGEMENTS

Mary Kibler, my wife and ministry partner for her suggestions, editing and support.

Jean Johnson, for her suggestions, editing and prayers.

Our Wonderful Church Family for their support and encouragement.

Our Partners whom I pray with every day.

All of God's people who know that nothing is more important than being born again.

If you have never received Jesus as your Savior, just pray this prayer and you will be saved.

Heavenly Father, I repent for all of my sins. I believe Jesus is the Son of God and He rose from the dead after suffering for my sins. Lord Jesus, please come into my heart and be my Savior and I will serve You for all of eternity.

If you just prayed this prayer you will spend eternity in Heaven with Jesus.

CONTENTS

INTRODUCTION

You are about to embark on a **life makeover** for the next 90 days that will change the course of your life and eventually bring you to a place of happiness, health, harmony and success.

No one has a choice of whether or not to live by their words, but everyone does have a choice of what words they will live by.

Words are the most powerful force that control and shape the lives of human beings.

Newton's first law of motion states that an object will remain at rest or in uniform motion in a straight line unless acted upon by an external force. God's law of motion, concerning our lives, might well be that a person's life will continue on the same course unless changed by words, spoken in faith.

THE SCRIPT FOR YOUR LIFE

Shakespeare said, "All the world is a stage, and all the men and women merely players." He could have added, that everyone will use their own words to write the script of their life.

Considering the power of the words that we speak **ABOUT OURSELVES**, we must learn to discipline ourselves concerning our speech. The words that WE SPEAK **ABOUT OURSELVES** have creative energy and incredible power.

The Bible refers to people who control their speech as being mature. Therefore, people who do not have control of their words are immature which means not fully developed. That was me for a long time.

So many people will say the first thing that comes to their mind without regard for the significance of what they are saying and later regret what they have said.

A wise person will weigh the consequences of what they are saying in any particular situation, because words matter. They can comfort people in time of grief, encourage people when they are discouraged and lift people up when they are emotionally drained. Or, inappropriate words can have exactly the opposite effect.

The most important words however, are the words that we say concerning **OURSELVES**. Because of that, the focus of this book is about ourselves and how to use our own words to create the life that we desire.

You will see the phrase, **ABOUT YOURSELF,** many times in this book, because the words you speak about other people, who are not under your authority, have very little or no ability to effect change. However, the words that you speak **ABOUT YOURSELF,** will have a huge effect on the direction of your life.

Hebrews 11:3 Through faith, we understand that God framed the worlds by His words.

God also created us with the creating ability to frame our world with our words and make no mistake about it, your words will frame your world. God will also never override the words that you speak **ABOUT YOURSELF.** God is not the final authority as to what happens in your life, you are.

The Bible tells us in James Chapter 3 that our tongue is like the rudder on a ship that the Captain uses to turn the ship around. Or, like a small bit in the mouth of a horse, that can easily turn the large animal around.

In this book you are going to learn how to frame your world, to steer your life, to get to the place you want to be in every area of your life. It is actually much easier than you might think. 90 Days from now, your life will be on a different course.

GIVING YOUR WORDS AN ASSIGNMENT

If you practice the simple principles outlined in this book, you will get to the point of actually giving your words an assignment to cause specific events or changes, to happen in your life. Not as difficult as you might think.

YOU WILL BECOME EMPOWERED

After reading this book you will be empowered to change any area of your life, any time you desire, in 90 days. You will absolutely be in charge of the destiny of your own life.

It is my wish that you will have a wonderful, happy, healthy and abundant life.

Read this book once a week for the first 90 days and at least once a month for the rest of your life after that. It is that important.

Give a copy of this book to everyone you know who needs a life makeover.

Say this out loud every day, "The rest of my life is the best of my life."

YOUR
WORDS MATTER

Have you ever noticed that people, who are living a horrible life, are usually saying horrible things **ABOUT THEMSELVES?** Did you ever think there might be a connection between their words and their life? Unfortunately, very few people realize that their lives are shaped and controlled by the words that they speak **ABOUT THEMSELVES.**

Everything that you say **ABOUT YOURSELF**, and believe, will happen. Spoken words go out into the spiritual realm and if left unchecked, will create changes, both good and bad, in the life of the person who spoke them.

Your life, over a period of time, will conform to the words that you speak **ABOUT YOURSELF** on a continual basis. This is true of everyone. No exceptions. The REAL SECRET is to make sure that you speak only positive words about yourself and eliminate the negative words.

Words have an incredible ability to help or hinder, to BLESS or curse, to cause sickness or health, or to bring poverty or wealth to any person.

Changing the words that you say about yourself, from negative to positive is a process, but over time will result in you living your life on a level you have only dreamed about.

CONTROL YOUR LIFE

If you can control your tongue, you have the ability to control all aspects of your life. Do not be deceived by how simple this is.

THE REAL LAW OF ATTRACTION

In the New Thought Philosophy, the law of attraction is the belief that by focusing on positive or negative thoughts, people can attract positive or negative experiences into their lives. Also, by doing this, they can attract into their lives money, friends, love, success, or anything else they desire.

The truth of the matter is, thoughts unspoken, have absolutely no magnetic power to attract, or create anything in your life. God created the world by **His Words** and we create our world by **our words**, both positive and negative.

By using positive words to create the life you desire, you are using the **REAL LAW OF ATTRACTION**, which, as you will see, is God's method of attracting good health, abundance, love and success into your life. Positive words have a magnetic effect on the lives of people.

WORDS IN THE SPIRITUAL REALM

When you speak words **ABOUT YOURSELF**, either positive or negative, those words go out into the spiritual realm and will continue to effect change for years. They can affect your family, and generations who follow, for hundreds of years or longer.

You can use words that you speak **ABOUT YOURSELF** to attract anything you desire into your life.

Mary and I once had a great need for something and we did not seem to be getting any closer to getting it. We were talking about it one day and all of a sudden I said, "You know, I spoke months ago that we would have that and those words are still out there and will bring it to us. She said, "That's right." The next day we got it.

Words spoken **ABOUT YOURSELF**, either positive or negative, unless nullified, will eventually accomplish their purpose.

REFUSE TO ACCEPT FAILURE

Refuse to accept defeat, failure, sickness or lack of any good thing in your life. What you are willing to accept in your life will never go away. People stay sick because they accept sickness. People stay broke because they believe that is the way it's meant to be for them. Do not fall into this trap. You are meant to live an abundant healthy life. Don't settle for anything less.

CHANGE YOUR THINKING

You can change negative thoughts into positive thoughts just by speaking positive words. The next time negative thoughts are going through your head about something, just start speaking positive words and statements out loud concerning what you were thinking about. Your thoughts will soon turn positive and be much more pleasant.

You will also increase your self-esteem simply by speaking only positive words **ABOUT YOURSELF.**

YOUR TONGUE STEERS YOUR LIFE

James 3:3-6 Behold, we put bits in the horses' mouths, that they may obey us; and we turn around their whole body.

⁴ Behold also the ships, which though they be so large, and are driven of fierce winds, yet are they turned around with a very small rudder, wherever the Captain wants it to go.

⁵ Even so the tongue is a little member and boast great things. Behold, how great a matter a little fire kindles!

⁶ And the tongue is a fire, a world of iniquity: so is the tongue among our members, that it can defile the whole body, and sets on fire the course of nature; and it is set on fire of hell.

Your tongue steers your life in the direction that you alone choose to go. The words that you speak **ABOUT YOURSELF** will determine the direction that your life takes in any given area. I call the tongue, a **steering wheel** for your life. Like it or not, believe it or not, every person's life is steered by their tongue.

CHOOSE YOUR WORDS CAREFULLY

The most powerful force in your life are the words that you **choose** to speak **ABOUT YOURSELF**.

Actually, every area of your life is subject to the words that you speak **ABOUT YOURSELF** in that particular area.

A person who does not control their words is like a driver going down the highway at 75 miles an hour, trying to steer the car while wearing a blindfold. Or like a marksman, trying to hit a target without aiming. You can use your tongue to aim your life in the direction that you want it to go.

When you change the words that you are saying **ABOUT YOURSELF**, from negative to positive, the complete turnaround will usually take 90 days before your life begins heading in the other direction.

YOUR TONGUE WORKS FOR YOU
OR AGAINST YOU

This is so simple. Make your tongue work for you, instead of against you, by changing the words you are speaking **ABOUT YOURSELF**. Your tongue can be your best friend, or worst enemy.

Decide what words you are going to speak in any given conversation, or situation. Everything will soon be under control and eventually have a good outcome.

GOD'S LAW OF WORDS

What would you think if God appeared to you and said, "From now on, everything you say **ABOUT YOURSELF** will come to pass?" Well, actually, that is exactly what God did say in Mark 11:23. Because of this, I would think you should be much more careful about what you say about yourself.

> **Mark 11:23 For truly I say unto you, that whosoever shall say unto this mountain, (Obstacle or Problem) be removed, and be cast into the sea; and shall not doubt in his heart but shall believe that those things which he says shall come to pass; <u>he shall have whatsoever he said.</u>**

The simple explanation of this verse is that if you speak to a hinderance, or obstacle, and tell it to leave your life it will, but **only if** you believe what you are saying. And if you say something concerning your own life, or something within your area of authority, **either good or bad** and believe it, you will get it.

Another explanation. Whatever you say **ABOUT YOURSELF** will come true, if you actually believe what you are saying.

This law applies to people speaking both positive and negative words **ABOUT THEMSELVES**. It also applies to people who believe what is in the Bible and people who don't. In other words, it applies to **EVERYBODY.**

If you say something **ABOUT YOURSELF** and do not believe it, nothing happens. You must believe what you say, without a doubt, in order for words to effect change. The trick is getting yourself to the point where you actually believe what you say. You are going to learn how to do that.

It seems to be more difficult to believe positive statements **ABOUT YOURSELF** than negative statements.

People have been conditioned to speak negatively, so it is much easier to believe negative statements.

FIRST WORDS

When something bad happens, the first thing that comes out of your mouth will determine the outcome of the situation because that is what you really believe.

Mary broke her arm several years ago and at the time our money was very tight. We had a 20% co pay on our insurance and naturally the bills all arrived at the same time. It amounted to over nine hundred dollars.

Mary was sitting at the table looking over the bills and she looked up at me and said, "We don't have enough money to pay these bills for my arm." I replied, "God will provide, now don't you say another word about it." She looked at me but said nothing. Within one month, we had enough money to pay all of those bills with money left over.

CLOSING YOUR MOUTH

Luke 1:13 But the angel said unto him, Fear not, Zacharias: for thy prayer is heard; and thy wife Elizabeth shall bear thee a son, and thou shalt call his name John.

Verse 18 and Zacharias said unto the angel, how shall I know this? For I am an old man, and my wife well stricken in years.

Verse 19 and the angel answering said unto him, I am Gabriel, that stands in the presence of God; and am sent to speak unto thee, and to show thee these glad tidings.

Verse 20 and, behold, <u>thou shall not be able to speak,</u> until the day that these things shall be performed, because you did not believe my words, which shall be fulfilled in their season.

Your words can and will override the Words of God concerning the plans He has for your life. God did not want Zacharias to ruin the plan that he had for his wife, Elizabeth, to give birth to John, the Baptist. That is why the angel shut the mouth of Zacharias when he said that his wife was too old to have the baby that God said they were going to have. Mary, my wife, calls this, spiritual duct tape. I keep a roll of duct tape by my pulpit at all times, to remind people to watch what they are saying **ABOUT THEMSELVES.**

AGREE WITH GOD'S WORD CONCERNING YOU

Luke 1:38 And Mary said, Behold the handmaid of the Lord; <u>be it unto me according to thy word</u>. And the angel departed from her.

Mary **agreed** with the Word of God when she was told that she would give birth to The Baby Jesus, even though she had never been with a man. Say the same thing that Mary said, concerning God's promises that pertain to you. There is something in the Bible concerning every situation that might ever arise in your life. Find it, agree with it out loud and watch what happens.

THE FLAPS ON THE SIDE OF YOUR HEAD

Mark 4: Jesus said, be careful what you hear.

I would add, or **who** you are listening to.

Guard the flaps on the side of your head, (Your ears). The words that go into your ears continually, both positive and negative will go down and begin to grow in your spirit. These words will eventually come out of your mouth and change your life. I absolutely do not allow people, who talk negatively, to spend time with me. **Stop giving negative people access to your ears!** I protect my ears from negative words.

If you feed your spirit, through your ears, with positive words **ABOUT YOURSELF** when you don't need them, your spirit will feed your mouth and cause it to speak positive words, when you do need them. When a situation then comes up you will find yourself speaking positive words about it and everything will soon work out in your favor.

WHAT YOU CONTINUALLY HEAR YOU WILL EVENTUALLY BELIEVE

You can only hear something a certain number of times before you begin to believe it. If you want someone to believe something, repeat it to them over and over again for months or even years if necessary and eventually they will believe it. This technique is called total immersion or brainwashing as it was used by Communist Countries to persuade people that their way of life was better than the alternative. They would tell people over and over how wonderful their way of life was, until they believed it. It was very effective. Politicians spend billions of dollars every four years to convince us that their ideas are better than that of their opponent's.

EARS ARE THE GATEWAY TO YOUR SPIRIT

The people you listen to actually have access to your spirit through your ears and will eventually, by the words they speak, cause changes to your life. This not only works for the person talking to you but also works through recordings and music. The truth of the matter is, you will begin to think like and become like the people you listen to.

If you are listening to good successful people, that can have a very good effect on your life. If they are bad, unsuccessful people, they can have a very bad effect on your life. Be very careful who you give access to your ears.

Decide who you want to be like and only listen to those people. I only listen to a certain group of people and I am becoming more like them every day. They are very anointed and successful. Who are you listening to??? If you do not want to become like a certain person do not listen to them or their recordings.

YOUR SPIRIT CAN OVERFLOW

Matthew 12:34 out of the abundance (Overflow) of the heart (Spirit) the mouth speaks.

The word abundance means overflow, or too much for your spirit to hold.

Your mouth is the overflow valve of your spirit or heart. It seems that the spirit of a person can only hold so many words, either good or bad, before they spill out of your mouth and makes changes in your life.

When you begin to listen to another person talk, either person to person or through recordings, nothing happens for a while. Eventually, your spirit becomes saturated or overloaded with what you are hearing and their words will begin to spill out of your mouth. That will soon cause you to start thinking like them, talking like them and becoming like them.

Never say, "My life sucks." Always say, "My life is great."

Never say, "My life is going nowhere." Always say, "I am moving up."

Never say, "No one likes me." Always Say, "Everyone likes me because I am a wonderful person."

Never Say, "Nothing ever works out for me." Always say, "Everything works out for me."

Never say, I am ugly." Always say, I am extremely good looking and getting better looking every day."

BLESSINGS
OR CURSES

James 3:10 Out of the same mouth comes blessing and cursing. My brethren, this should not be so.

Everything you say **ABOUT YOURSELF**, either BLESSES your life or curses your life. Make sure that you are not cursing yourself as most people do on a daily basis.

CHOOSE LIFE OR DEATH

Deuteronomy 30:19 I call heaven and earth to record this day against you, that I have set before you, life and death, blessing and cursing: therefore, choose life, that both <u>you and your descendants</u> may live.

According to The Bible, life or death and BLESSING and cursing are all choices. There are two aspects of this. The first is life, if we accept the terms of God's Covenant, and death if we do not.

Also, according to the New Testament, we choose life if we accept Jesus as our Savior and Spiritual Death if we do not.

The second, is the fact that we can choose BLESSINGS and reject curses.

This verse also mentions descendants, which means that choices can be generational. The choice of words that you speak during this lifetime can affect your descendants for years to come. Be careful.

POWER OF THE TONGUE

Proverbs 18:21 Your tongue has the power of life and death over you and you will live by the words that come out of your mouth.

Your tongue has absolutely incredible power over your life and you will live by the words that you speak. All of us can have life, if we control our tongue regarding ourselves, and death if we do not.

HOW CURSES GET STARTED

Genesis 9:25 and Noah said to his son, cursed be Canaan; a servant of servants shall he be unto his brethren.

Curses do not just happen, they must be voice activated by someone in authority. Very few people realize that negative things we say today, to and about our children, are actually curses and can affect them and our grandchildren for hundreds of years. Are you inadvertently cursing your children? This is one way that generational curses get started.

A spoken word goes out into the spiritual realm and can affect and control situations and circumstances indefinitely.

Many people are living under curses that have been spoken over them either by themselves, parents or ancestors. This is a major reason for sickness and poverty and lack in families, and in the lives of people. These can easily be broken. If you do not know how to break these curses, call me because I help people with this every day.

HOW BLESSINGS GET STARTED

Genesis 28 and give thee the Blessing of Abraham to you and your seed.

Words we speak now **ABOUT OURSELVES,** or our children, have the potential to affect things in our families for years to come.

Read Genesis Chapters 27 and 28. This is the story of Jacob and how his father spoke a BLESSING over him. Afterwards he went to his uncle's house to live and work. His uncle cheated him, deceived him and lowered his wages 10 times. Jacob nevertheless became rich and finally became the owner of almost all of his uncle's herds.

All parents should speak BLESSINGS over their children every day and their children will become successful. When my son was little, I always said to him, "You are a good boy and a smart boy." That is exactly how he was when growing up and how he turned out as an adult.

The words you speak now, either BLESSINGS or curses, can affect your family for thousands of years to come. It has been 4,000 years since Isaac spoke THE BLESSING over Jacob in Genesis 28:4 when He said, "And give thee the BLESSING OF ABRAHAM to thee and to thy seed with thee." This BLESSING still affects the lives of all Jewish people and all born again people who receive it, including me.

THE PASTOR'S BLESSING

Pastors are commanded by God, in **Numbers 6:22-27**, to speak a WORD FOR WORD BLESSING over the people in their church on a regular basis.

> **The Lord Bless You and Keep You.**
>
> **The Lord make His Face shine upon you.**
>
> **The Lord lift up His Countenance upon you and give you peace.**

These are God's Words and He wants them spoken over His people, word for word. Does your Pastor do this? If not, why not?

SPEAK BLESSINGS OVER PETS

Call your dog good and smart and you will have a good and smart dog. How many people have you ever heard call their dog stupid? If you call your dog stupid you will have a stupid dog.

On the way home, the day we bought Muffy, Mary and I spoke over her. We said, "She is a good dog, a wonderful dog, a smart dog and will be the perfect dog for us." Thirteen years later that is still exactly how she is. She has never been disciplined or even scolded. She has been and is still a perfect pet for us. Muffy is precious to us and very much loved.

BLESS YOURSELF

Every time you speak positive words **ABOUT YOURSELF** you are actually blessing yourself and those words will cause good things to happen in your life unless they are nullified.

Never say, "I must be cursed." Always say, "I am BLESSED.

Never say, "I'll be damned." Always say, I'll be BLESSED."

Never say, "My kid is stupid and will never amount to anything." Always say, "My children are smart and will be successful at everything they do."

Men, always say, "My wife is beautiful, smart and very talented."

Women, always say, "I have a wonderful husband and He is handsome, smart and successful."

HEALTH OR SICKNESS

You can actually use positive words to heal yourself of sickness and disease as your body will respond to positive words that you speak about it.

A huge factor in whether or not a person lives a healthy life, is the words that they speak concerning their health.

Mary and I knew a wonderful couple who were very wealthy but had no control of their words, especially concerning their health. One or the other or sometimes both, were sick almost all the time. One day the lady said to us, "My husband is better now so I guess it's my turn to get sick." They took turns getting sick. Soon afterwards, the husband got sick again and this time he died.

A HEALED HEART

A lady from our church, Jean, was diagnosed five years ago with congestive heart failure. She was given between one month and a year to live. She could not walk more than thirty feet without stopping to catch her breath.

I took Jean to the doctor and he told us that she had congestive heart failure and that her heart was only working at about 40%.

He also said that she would not get any better and that he was just trying to keep her out of the hospital. She was very discouraged and for that matter so was I.

When we got home she sat down on the couch and I went back to the office. All of a sudden I got up, came out and stood in front of her and said, "We are not going to go by what the doctor said. From now on, every day we are going to say your heart is strong and getting stronger every day." Then I said, "Your heart is strong and getting stronger every day." Jean said, "My heart is strong and getting stronger every day."

We said this every morning for three months (90 days) and nothing changed. However, sometime during the 4th month, Mary and I decided to take Muffy for a walk and Jean said, "I am coming with you." She walked all the way down to the end of the block, rested and walked back. I said to Mary, "She is getting better."

We went back to the doctor and he said, "I just don't understand this, congestive heart failure does not improve but the walls of your heart have become thinner and your heart is pumping fine." Of course, we told him what we had done. She is back to work and living a normal, very productive life and is a key part of this ministry. She had used positive words for 90 days to heal what the doctors had said, was a terminal heart condition.

If you have a major disease that is hindering your life, say, "By the stripes of Jesus I was healed" 100 times a day for 90 days and watch what happens.

SUICIDE BY TONGUE

A few years ago, there was a wonderful woman in our church who had been miraculously healed of pancreatic cancer. She was totally cancer free for over two years but would not stop talking about how weak and sick she was, even though her health was fine. Finally, cancer came back in another area of her body and she died a horrible death. She had used negative words about her health, as a weapon to kill herself. Do you know anyone who is using their tongue to slowly commit suicide? I'll bet you do.

GENERATIONAL CURSES OF SICKNESS

Many times, at the root of sickness and disease is a generational curse that has been running in a family for years. Doctors call diseases that run through families, hereditary. The truth of the matter is that any disease that runs in families is a generational curse which, in all probabilities, had been spoken by someone years ago.

Generational curses of sickness can be started as easily as someone saying, "My kids get sick all the time." Or, "Everyone in my family has a bad heart." Or, "Breast cancer runs in my family."

Examples of generational curses of sickness are:

Heart disease

Cancer

Arthritis

Diabetes

High Blood Pressure

And Many More

Be careful that you do not start a generational curse of sickness in your family.

SAY THE OPPOSITE

Joel 3:10 Let the weak say I am strong.

If there is anything wrong with you mentally or physically, say just the opposite. If at any time I do not feel good I will say, "I don't feel good but I am getting better." Words about your health, spoken in the present or the past will not harm you. Just be very careful about speaking in future tense.

So many people will cause a health problem to get worse by constantly making statements like, my legs are getting weaker all the time, I can't eat this or that, my back hurts all the time, my eyes are getting worse, I don't sleep well, I have this or that. You get the picture. The condition of these people will continue to get worse.

They did a large study several years ago and found that people who rated their health as poor were almost three times as likely to die during the seven years of the study than people who rated their health as excellent. What are you saying about your health?

INCREASE YOUR INTELLIGENCE

Would you like to be smarter? You absolutely can.

I use to be a terrible speller but after 90 days of saying "I am smart and getting smarter every day, I could spell just about any word.

I flunked high school chemistry because I just did not understand anything that was going on in that class. One evening, I picked up my stepson's college chemistry book and spent the entire evening reading through it. I understood everything perfectly and if I took that college class today my grade would most definitely be an A.

WHY SO MANY PEOPLE GET THE FLU

How many times have you heard people say, "We get the flu every year when it comes around?" I can tell you right now that those people will get the flu every year. Start saying, "We never get the flu at our house."

THE MAJOR CAUSE OF DEMENTIA.

I guarantee you that 99% of the people with dementia started this process by saying things like, "I can't remember things like I used to, I am getting so forgetful, I forget things all the time." Instead, if you forget something, say, "I will remember it because I never forget anything, my mind is quick and sharp and I am getting smarter every day." The wellbeing of your brain depends on your words.

HOW YOUR BRAIN RESPONDS TO WORDS

The human brain responds much faster to negative words than to positive words. The reason is because negative words are perceived by the brain as a threat to survival. Any threat to survival, perceived or real, causes acute stress and the body is not able to function properly or rest.

Positive words propel the motivational center of the brain and also help to build resilience when problems arise. They are also shown to significantly lower both physical and emotional stress.

DEVELOP A STRONG SPIRIT

Proverbs 18:14 The Spirit of a person will sustain their sickness but no one can bear up under a weak spirit.

Every time you speak positive words, **ABOUT YOURSELF**, your spirit gets stronger and a strong spirit will sustain you through any health issues. Negative words will weaken your spirit and a weak spirit will not help you at all during any adversity.

A SIMPLE CURE FOR DEPRESSION

Negative words produce negative thoughts which lead to stress, fear, anxiety, worry, and finally depression. Every time you feel depressed, force yourself to say positive things about your situation, even if you don't believe it. Do this until the depression leaves. You may be surprised because it won't take long.

NEVER USE THESE WORDS

The strongest stress producing words are the words NO and CAN'T. When used with the word I in the same sentence, such as saying, "I can't" or "No I can't" you are conveying a message to the brain that something is impossible for you to accomplish. This produces stress and a sense of failure.

You should absolutely never use the word **CAN'T** when talking **ABOUT YOURSELF** as this word will greatly diminish your capabilities. The rule of thumb is, when you say, "I can't," you can't. The opposite is also true. If you say, "I can," you can. No matter how difficult the task at hand is, just keep saying, "I can do this" and I guarantee you will eventually do it.

Never say, "I get sick all the time." Always say, "I never get sick."

Never say, "I am weak." Always say, "I am getting stronger every day"

Never say, I can't get over this cold." Always Say "I am getting better every day."

Never say, "I can't remember things anymore." Always say, 'I never forget anything because my mind is quick and sharp."

Never Say, "I am getting old." Always say "I am getting younger every day."

Never say, "My health is poor." Always say, "My health is excellent." No matter what the condition of your health happens to be.

Never say, "I am so dumb." Always say, "I am smart and getting smarter every day."

SUCCESS OR FAILURE

You can use your own words to create a successful life for yourself.

Success does not mean the same thing to everyone. To me, the definition of success is a person who is stress free and happy, who likes themselves, is living the life they truly want and feel that they deserve. I would also add in my case, doing what I want to do, where I want to do it and with the people I want to do it with, making progress and learning new things every day.

Proverbs 13:20 The person who walks with wise people will be wise but a companion of fools shall be destroyed.

Success requires having a mindset that strives for success. Successful people talk differently and think differently than unsuccessful people. Associate with them and you will begin to talk like them, think like them, act like them and be like them. If you associate with unsuccessful people you will become like them. In today's vernacular, if you hang out with fools you will become a fool.

TALK LIKE SUCCESSFUL PEOPLE TALK

When I would join a new sales company the first thing I would look for is the top sales people and those are the people I would try to make friends with. In any organization, the top 20% do 80% of the business. Also 20% of the people own 80% of the wealth in almost all free countries. This is called the Pareto Principle (80/20 rule). Hang out with the top 20% and you will begin to talk like them and sooner than you think, you will become one of them.

CHANGE YOUR THINKING

If you have been unsuccessful, the first step toward achieving success is to renew your mind, to change the way you perceive yourself. You must begin to see yourself as being successful in every area of your life. This begins with changing your words. Start by saying, "I am successful, I am the best at what I do, I am happy and there is nothing I can't do."

THE DIFFERENCE

Over one million kids play high school football each year and I am sure that every one of them would love to someday play in the NFL. A lot of these kids are very talented but sad to say, only about one in five hundred will ever make it to the NFL level. What is the difference, you ask?

Have you ever watched NFL players being interviewed? Every one of them believes in their heart that they are better than anyone else at what they do. They talk and act like they are God's gift to football. It takes this kind of mindset to be successful at the NFL level. They believe they are special and that they are supposed to be there, doing what they are doing. They are right on all accounts. I have never heard a NFL player say anything negative about himself.

Adopt this same attitude. <u>Quietly</u> apply these same principles to your job or profession and watch what happens. You will quickly rise to the top.

As you regularly speak words of success about yourself, negative thoughts of doubt about yourself and your abilities will gradually fade, and you will become successful.

PERSONALITY MAKEOVER

Everyone likes people who have good personalities. Speak positive words about everything and everyone. Do not be disagreeable. Make an effort to be pleasant. You will be amazed by how fast people will begin to be drawn to your new personality.

HOW TO BE HAPPY

Happiness starts with a decision. Make a decision to be happy and start saying, "I am a happy person and people like me." Do this every day for 90 days and you will genuinely be much happier and people will like you.

HOW TO QUIT SMOKING

Most people fail when they try to stop smoking. The easy way to stop smoking is that every time you light up a cigarette just say out loud, "I do not desire to smoke." If you do this **every time** you light up, your desire to smoke will leave and you will stop smoking in 90 days with no pills and no patches.

HOW TO LOSE WEIGHT

We all know that diets do not work. The truth of the matter is that if you take into your body less calories than you need, you will lose weight and if you take in more than you need, you will gain weight. The answer is take in less.

The way to do this is simple. Every time you sit down to eat, before you take a bite say, "I do not desire to over eat.' Do this for 90 days and the weight will begin to come off. A man in Arkansas did this and lost 120 pounds.

HOW TO BECOME BETTER LOOKING

Ladies, look in the mirror every day and say "I am getting more beautiful every day." In 90 days, everyone else will agree with you and people will turn their heads to look at you. Men, every day say, "I am getting better looking every day." Do this for 90 days and watch what happens.

HOW TO SLEEP GOOD AT NIGHT

How many people have you heard say "I don't sleep well at night." Guess what? They will never sleep well at night if they keep talking like that. If you want a good night's sleep, just start saying, "I sleep good at night." Say this on a regular basis and very soon you will sleep like a baby,

Never say, "Nothing I ever do works out." Always say, "Everything works out for me."

Never say, "Tomorrow is going to be a hard day." Always say, "Tomorrow will be better than today"

Never say, "I hate my job." Always say, "I love my job and I work for a great company."

Never say, I am such a loser." Always say, I am very successful at everything I do."

Never say, "I can't do anything right." Always say, I can do anything."

Never say, "I am so unhappy." Always say, "I am a happy person."

Always say, "I am a wonderful person, I have a great personality and I am happy all the time."

POVERTY
OR PROSPERITY

Proverbs 10:15 The rich person's wealth is their protection: the poverty of poor people is destruction.

Poverty causes destruction. It tears apart families and causes unbelievable stress in the lives of wonderful people. Not having enough money to live on and pay your bills is a terrible thing as many of you very well know. Positive words for 90 days will begin to turn your finances around.

Have you ever listened to how most poor people talk **ABOUT THEMSELVES**? Many of them are constantly cursing themselves concerning their finances.

Most poor people have been conditioned to despise people who are well off. They refer to them as "The other half." I love rich people because they are the ones who provide the jobs. I have never been hired for a job by a poor person. The rule of thumb is, you will never become like the people you despise.

If you want to become prosperous, don't complain about prosperous people, do what prosperous and successful people do and start talking like them.

GENERATIONAL CURSE OF POVERTY

It seems that there is a spirit of poverty flowing through poor families, because most poor people do come from poor families.

Deuteronomy 28:29 and you shalt grope at noonday, as the blind gropes in darkness, and you shall not prosper in thy ways: and you shall be only oppressed and spoiled <u>forever</u>, and no person shall be able to help you.

This is the generational curse of poverty and lack and unless it is broken, people will struggle financially no matter how hard they work. It can be overcome by speaking positive words **ABOUT YOURSELF** concerning your finances.

THE WAR ON POVERTY

According to the Cato Institute, about 15 trillion dollars has been given to poor people in the form of welfare by the United States Government since President Johnson declared "War on poverty' in 1964. Another 7 trillion dollars has been spent on anti-poverty programs for a total investment in fighting poverty of 23 Trillion dollars. The poverty rate is the same now as it was then. It would certainly seem that money and programs are not the answer to fighting poverty.

IT'S NOT ABOUT MONEY

Neither prosperity or poverty are about money, it's about a mindset. If you took all the money away from all the rich people and gave it all to poor people, within one year, the rich people would be rich again and the poor people would be poor again.

Years ago, I knew a Jewish man who invested all of his money and all that he could borrow from family and friends in a nightclub. Within three months he was out of business and broke. He and his wife came over to visit soon after and I said, "John, I am so sorry, what are you going to do?" He replied, "It's just money, I'll get it back." He was not even concerned because he knew his success did not depend on money or any one business venture.

MCDONALD'S

The first McDonald's fast food restaurant opened in 1948. They became very successful during the next 15 years. People began to take notice and soon fast food restaurants began springing up all over the country. Other people started selling hamburgers the same way. Then chicken, roast beef, fish, pizza followed. A lot of people made a lot of money marketing food exactly the same way. Copy a successful formula for business and you will be successful.

Whatever business you want to go into, find successful people doing the same thing, copy their method of operation and if possible, learn to talk like them.

If it's not Broke, Don't Fix it.

Many people will make changes to a successful program and then cry when things change for the worse.

IF IT DOESN'T WORK, CHANGE IT QUICKLY.

I have known so many people who were in trouble in their businesses and keep doing the same thing until they went broke. Years ago, Mary and I took over a restaurant that had very little business. At first, we also had very few customers but we constantly made changes until we found the right concept and menu. We were also saying, "We have a great business." Soon we had a great business. The rule is, if what you are doing is not working, SAY SOMETHING DIFFERENT AND DO SOMETHING DIFFERENT!

Never say, "Times are hard." Always say, "Times are always good for me."

Never say, "It's tough to make money these days." Always say, "Money comes easy to me."

Never say, "Everything I touch turns to garbage." Always say, Everything I touch turns to gold."

Never say, "I can't afford this." Always say "I can have anything I want."

Never say, I am broke." Always say, "I will never be broke another day in my life."

90 DAY
TURN AROUND

Abraham changed his words, at the age of 100, from negative to positive. His wife was 90, at the time, and they had no faith for the baby that God had promised them. God changed his name from Abram to Abraham which means father of many people. He was then forced to call himself father of many people, which at the time he was not.

90 days later this resulted in his 90-year-old wife getting pregnant. Can you imagine what will happen to you if you change your words for 90 days? Change your words for 90 days and your life will also turn around!

Just because God says something about you, does not mean that it is going to happen. You must also say it yourself and believe it.

A 90 DAY PROCESS

Genesis 17:4 Neither shall thy name any more be called Abram, but thy name shall be Abraham; for a father of many nations have I made thee.

Even though God had said that he was the father of many nations, nothing happened until Abraham himself said that he was a father of many nations and finally believed what he said. That process took 90 days. Changing your life is also a process that will take up to 90 days.

No matter what the circumstances look like, keep speaking positive words. It may take 90 days but things will begin to change for the better.

Speaking positive words about yourself is not only a process, it is a way of life.

If Abraham can change his words **ABOUT HIMSELF** from negative to positive and 90 days later his 90-year-old wife gets pregnant, you can surely turn your life around in 90 days. HUH?

If you say only positive things about yourself, your health, your finances, your life, your circumstances and situation for 90 days, without saying anything negative, you will begin to notice a difference. If you keep doing it for one year your life will change. If you keep it up for five years you will be living your life on a level you never imagined.

HOW MY LIFE TURNED AROUND

Mary and I struggled for years to pay our bills. We would have to use all the faith we had just to make our rent payments at the end of each month. Finally, about 10 years ago, I got a revelation that the problem was me. I was speaking negative words concerning my finances.

I decided to see how long I could go without saying anything negative **ABOUT MYSELF**. I bought a calendar and the plan was to give myself a check mark for each day that I did not say anything bad **ABOUT MYSELF**. After several tries, I finally had a whole week of check marks. Then a whole month. Can you imagine going one whole month without speaking any negative words **ABOUT YOURSELF**? But nothing changed, we were still struggling to pay our bills at the end of the first month.

Then two months went by without any negative words about myself. Still broke.

Then three months and now I really had something going but we were still struggling to pay our bills. Nevertheless, I decided to see how long I could keep this going.

However, the forth month was much different. Extra money began to come in from different directions. At the end of four months we had money left over and we have had money left over at the end of every month since the 90 days. We have never struggled to pay our bills since that time. Our bank account began to grow. All the stress left our life and has never returned.

The key to our finances was definitely eliminating negative words about ourselves. Our finances and our whole lives had turned around in only 90 Days.

GETTING YOUR WORDS
UNDER CONTROL

Put yourself on the same program. Get a Calendar and before you go to bed, give yourself a check mark if you have not said anything negative about yourself all day. Negative thoughts do not count against you unless you speak them.

> **James 1:19 Wherefore, my beloved brethren, let every person be swift to hear, slow to speak, slow to become angry.**

The key to this program is simple. Before you say anything **ABOUT YOURSELF**, think about what you are saying. Weigh your words carefully and speak very slow **ABOUT YOURSELF**.

If you do not control your words they will destroy you. If you do control your words, they will enrich every area of your life immeasurably.

If you eliminate negative words **ABOUT YOURSELF**, the only words that will come out of **YOUR** mouth, **ABOUT YOU,** are positive words.

This is a process. Do not get discouraged if at first if you have a hard time with this. You can do it, ANYONE CAN. It gets much easier as you go along and before you know it, watching your words will become second nature to you.

THE KEY TO CHANGING THINGS

> **Genesis 17:4 God said to Abraham, as it is written, I have made thee a father of many nations, before him whom**

he believed, even God, who quickens the dead, and calls those things which be not as though they were.

The key to this program is the fact that: **what you continually hear you will eventually believe,** whether you are saying it, or you are hearing someone else say it. Then when you finally say it and believe it you get it.

Speaking the opposite of what you actually have is the scriptural law of ATTRACTING something into your life. This works every time, if you keep at it for 90 days. If you call things that are, the way they are, they will stay the way they are, or get worse.

God's method of changing things is to call things that be not as though they are until it happens. I tell people, "If you want something bad enough, call it as though it were 100 times a day for 90 days. This of course depends on your determination factor. If you cannot pay your bills, or if you are sick, your determination factor should be high. Try saying "I have plenty of money" 100 times a day for 90 days and see what happens. How easy is this?

You can change any area of your life by changing your words regarding that area for 90 days.

ABRAHAM CALLED THINGS THAT WERE NOT AS THOUGH THEY WERE FOR 90 DAYS.

I guarantee you that when Abraham started calling himself father of many people, he did not believe it. But after doing this for 90 days he believed what he was saying and his 90-year-old wife became pregnant. He called something that was not as though it was. What can you say about yourself for 90 days?

UNDER YOUR NOSE

The answer to all of your problems in right under your nose. You can actually use your mouth to solve your problems and change your situations and circumstances.

PAID OFF HOUSE

Several years ago, we owed twice as much on a house as it was worth. We had financed it at the peak of the housing boom and then the bottom dropped out and the houses in our area were worth half as much.

One night after midnight I went out into the street, pointed my finger at the house and said out loud, "In the Name of Jesus, I call you sold and it will not cost us any money." Every time I thought about it I said, "Our house is sold." Two years later the house sold and it did not cost us one penny.

BE SLOW TO AGREE WITH ANYONE

If someone says something and you agree with them, it is the same as you saying it about yourself.

One time, before church I overheard two people talking in the children's area. One person said, "Well, it's just one thing after another." The other person replied, "It sure is." I knew they were BOTH in for one thing after another.

A few years ago, our next-door neighbor and his wife, who were absolutely wonderful Christian people, were leaving their home, of 55 years, to move into an assisted living facility. They were both very sad about leaving.

He came over to say good bye and said to me, "Well Jim, this is going to happen to all of us." I did not reply. He said it again and again I did not reply. He looked at me directly and said it a third time. I looked back at him and as gently as I could, said, "You are a wonderful person and we love you both, but that is not going to happen to us."

He was offended and I felt very bad but if I had agreed with him, the same thing would have eventually happened to us. I was not going to let that happen to Mary and me, even at the expense of losing a friendship.

Proverbs 13:20 He that associates with wise people shall be wise: but a companion of fools shall be destroyed.

This verse is very important because everyone will soon act like and talk like the people they hang out with. Stop hanging out with negative people. Almost everyone will agree that every problem they have ever had in their lives was because of the people they were associated with or were in a relationship with. Why do you think your mother was always concerned about the people you had for friends? She was concerned that you would become like them.

CHURCH CAN BE A DANGEROUS PLACE

Several years ago, Mary and I were visiting a large church with a very well-known Pastor. About half way through the sermon he said, "Trouble is going to come to you." People said amen all over the building. I said out loud, "Not to me it isn't." Almost everyone in our area turned around and looked at me. I said, "I am not going to agree with that." I said to Mary, "Everyone who said amen to that should duck because trouble is coming at them right now." Be careful when you say amen in church. If you agree with what someone else says, and believe it, you will get it. Be very careful about agreeing with other people about anything even in church.

When people I am talking to say anything negative about themselves I will not reply, or just say, "**If you say so.**"

THE WORD CYCLE

Galatians 6:7 Do not be deceived, God is not mocked: everyone will reap exactly what they sow.

Mark 4:14 The sower sows the word.

When you speak words **ABOUT YOURSELF** either positive or negative they go into your ear and are sown or planted down into your spirit.

When you keep sowing these words, the words keep growing, and soon will begin to come out of your mouth back into your ear and down into your spirit again.

Each time the words cycle they become stronger until they start changing your life. The words in your spirit will continually grow, come out of your mouth and eventually produce dramatic changes in your life. If you speak some positive words and some negative words, it's like weeds growing with the flowers. If you keep planting weeds in your spirit they will soon choke the good words.

PICK YOUR AREA

To start with, decide which area of your life you want to improve first, your personality, or health or finances or anything else you desire. Direct positive words toward that area intensely for 90 days and you will begin to notice changes.

I CAN HELP YOU "IF"

I tell people who call my Prayer Line, "**If** you watch your words I can help you get healed or to receive THE BLESSING OF GOD upon your life. **If** you don't watch your words, there is nothing I can do to help you."

CONTROL YOUR FUTURE

If you control your words and say only positive words that are well chosen, you can control your future and guide your life in the direction you want to go. Anyone can do this. **YOU CAN DO THIS! Start today.**

Never say, "My life is terrible." Always say, "My life is getting better every day."

Never say, "Everything is hard for me." Always say "Everything is easy for me."

Never say, "Nothing ever works out for me." Always say, "Everything works out for me."

Never say, "I can't get out of debt." Always say, "My debt is going away."

Never say, "I have no friends because no one likes me." Always say, "I am a wonderful person and everyone likes me."

ABOUT THE AUTHOR

Pastor Jim Kibler was born in Pittsburgh and grew up in Slippery Rock, Pennsylvania. He is a graduate of Mount St. Mary's College in Emmitsburg, Maryland, and Rhema Bible College in Tulsa, Oklahoma. He also did graduate work in business at George Washington University in Washington, DC.

Pastor Jim and his wife Mary, who is also a graduate of Rhema Bible College, Pastor <u>Life Church</u> in Indialantic, Florida.

Pastor Jim's popular website is www.increasenow.com, a **FREE SITE**, where people around the world watch his FREE 15 Minute videos every day. He teaches about God's Goodness, Healing, Redemption, Abundance and The Blessing.

Also watch Pastor Jim's live broadcast every day by downloading the free Periscope App on your phone and follow Pastor Jim Kibler.

FOLLOW PASTOR JIM KIBLER ON FACEBOOK AND INSTAGRAM

In addition, Pastor Jim is a Very Entertaining Conference Speaker and everywhere he speaks, people get healed, finances increase and churches grow. He makes God's Word very easy to understand. He also has a very anointed healing ministry with people being healed of every type of disease and blind eyes opened.

Pastor Jim has a wonderful Prayer Ministry and makes himself available to pray with people who do not have a Pastor to pray with them. He is Personal Pastor to many people who otherwise do not have a Pastor to Talk to, Speak THE BLESSING over them, or Pray the Prayer of Faith for their needs.

His Prayer Ministry has had incredible results. Many people are healed right over the phone, have the curse of the law and generational curses broken and have THE BLESSING activated in their lives.

Pastor Jim's phone number is available at www.increasenow.com

He is called the **"How To Preacher"** because he not only teaches people what God has promised, but how to receive it.

Other Books by Pastor Jim:

"How To Pray"

"The Blessing"

"Jesus"

"If the Bible Is True"

54056708R00035

Made in the USA
Columbia, SC
26 March 2019